A POCKETFUL OF MEMORIES

WAR MEMORIES

(RECOLLECTIONS & STORIES)

Edited By
GREG STOKES

THE KATES HILL PRESS

First Published By THE KATES HILL PRESS
126 Watsons Green Road, Kates Hill, Dudley, DY2 7LG

My War Memories. Copyright © Sylvia Thomas 2007
Recollection of the War Years. Copyright © Tossie Parick 2007
The Evacuees. Copyright © Edna Mitchell 2007
The Long Shift, and Lock Out. Copyright © Greg Stokes 2007

ISBN: 978 1 904552 18 5

British Library CIP Data:
A catalogue record for this book is available
from the British Library

This book is sold subject to the condition that it
shall not, by way of trade or otherwise, be lent,
resold, hired out or otherwise circulated without
the publisher's prior consent in any form or binding
other than that in which it is published.

Printed By: Print Services Unit, University of Wolverhampton

Cover Design By: Greg Stokes

A POCKETFUL OF MEMORIES - WAR MEMORIES
(RECOLLECTION & STORIES)

Sylvia Thomas:
My War Memories   5

Tossie Patrick:
Recollection of the War Years   22

Greg Stokes:
The Long Shift   33
(An adaptation of a war story told by Wilf Hackett)
Lock Out   39
(An adaptation of a war story told by Irene M Davies)

Edna Mitchell:
The Evacuees   43

RECOLLECTIONS

SYLVIA THOMAS was born and brought up in the west end of Dudley. She originally wrote her war memories for younger members of her own family in attempt to show them what it was like to live through the conflict. However, she went on to present the piece in schools. My War Memories has been on the Kates Hill Press website for a few years now and is one of the most frequently visited items.

TOSSIE PATRICK, author of A Pocketful of Memories - Blackheath, continues bringing the past to life with her recollections of the war as it affected the town, and a young women in work.

EDNA MITCHELL lived out in Wilnecote near Tamworth, very much a rural setting on the fringes of the west midlands conurbation. Much has been written about evacuees from their viewpoint. Edna recalls the evacuees coming to her community.

STORIES

GREG STOKES has written two stories to accompany these recollections.

Greg spent many hours round at author CLARICE HACKETT's house. Her husband Wilf used to tell a tale of the time he had to work all weekend in the war. THE LONG SHIFT is based on that tale.

In May 2006 Greg took IRENE M DAVIES, author of A Pocketful of Memories Rowley, to Birmingham to appear on the Carl Chinn Show. On the way back she told him of her time at the Button during the war. The story is reproduced here as LOCK OUT.

MY WARTIME MEMORIES

A few months ago my grandchildren were quizzing me on what happened to me and what were my experiences during the Second World War. My daughter was also listening and later suggested that I should write down all these experiences otherwise in years to come no one would ever know. Having thought it over, I decided it would not be a bad idea despite the fact that I am no author. This will not be a story of heroism or direct endurance under blitz conditions, but an ordinary recollection of an ordinary girl growing into womanhood under war conditions. Obviously I will be unable to cover the whole period in detail from 1939-1945, but will relate incidents that stand out in my memory. So here goes.

I was twelve and a half years old when war was declared but I can clearly recall the actual declaration. My parents, sister and Uncle Albert (a courtesy uncle) were together in the kitchen and the wireless as it was referred to then (now referred to as the radio) was on, when the announcement was made. After Mr. Chamberlain had finished, there was a stunned silence and I believe it was me who asked what would happen. I recall Uncle Albert saying that our newly acquired kitten (born the previous July) would have to go, which greatly upset my sister and I and our concern was principally about 'Tibby' the kitten. What Uncle Albert really meant was that there would not be enough food to feed the kitten. How wrong he was because 'Tibby' lived until 1951!

During the next few weeks it was rather quiet, my parents were busy preparing our cellar in readiness for any air raids, because having a cellar we did not qualify for an Anderson Air Raid Shelter. Around the cellar was a wide brick shelf in the shape of an 'L', standing about two feet from the floor. Dad boarded up the one end to hold the coal behind, this was nearest the street so that any further deliveries could be poured down the 'coal hole'. Dad then cleaned the remainder of the 'L' shape shelf and then laid straw upon it. The 'L' was split which made two narrow beds and on these spaces he placed the feather beds brought down from our bedrooms. Bed linen and pillows completed the job and hey presto, two very comfy beds. The main drawback that made me detest these beds were spiders (which I loathed) and other damp loving insects. The floor of the cellar was covered with boards and placed on these were whatever rugs and mats that could be spared. There were also two chairs and a small table upon which was a supply of candles and a candleholder in the event of a cut in the electricity supply. This was to be our sanctuary for many months together with neighbours who lived in 'cottages' at the back of our house. In a very short time they decided to stay in their Cottages and ignored the air raids.

Another precaution in the event of air raids was to try to prevent flying glass and this was achieved by putting sticky brown tape in patterns across the glass. Needless to say, many of these patterns took the form of the stripes in the national flag better known as the 'Union Jack'. When the sticky tape became scarce, old lace curtains were used by immersing them in glue and then applied to the windows.

Ration books were issued for everyone, as were gas masks. I hated having to wear the latter because I felt so closed in; in fact, these were probably to blame in later years when I discovered I suffered from claustrophobia. The smell of rubber was horrible. These masks were issued in cardboard boxes which had to accompany you wherever you went and it was not long before home made covers were invented for these boxes to protect them from inclement weather and were made from whatever material was available, the most popular of which was leather with leather straps for carrying. We did not carry the gas masks around with us for the whole duration of wartime; we became rather blasé and soon left them at home.

Another result of wartime was the removal of all signposts. This was done in case of invasion to prevent invaders knowing where they were, or which way to go to any specific destination. This was very confusing to anyone unfamiliar with any district and to ask a passer-by for directions was treated with great suspicion because of the existence of what was termed 'the Fifth Column'. This 'Fifth Column' apparently consisted of Nazi sympathizers (some smuggled in from Germany) who infiltrated anywhere where information could be gathered, hence the slogans that were invented 'careless talk costs lives' and 'walls have ears'.

If, by any chance, you lived in a house that had spare bedrooms, you would find that the authorities would 'billet' people on you and you would not be able to avoid this ruling. The 'billeted' people could either be a member or members of the armed forces, or a member or members of Government Departments or a 'Bevin' boy or boys. The latter were men who were conscripted into working in the coal mines, a very worthy job which not nearly enough credit was given and many men were transferred miles away from their homes, hence the need to 'billet' them. Even if you were of the so-called 'upper class' and owned a large house, quite often these were requisitioned for use by the armed services or as hospitals.

Paper was in short supply too, because wood for pulping had to be brought from abroad and only essential war supplies were transported by sea, which was extremely dangerous for both our Naval forces and the gallant men of our Merchant Navy, whose ships very often were without guns or any means of defending themselves. All paper was very carefully used, one way was to use 'economy labels', these were sticky labels to affix to used envelopes in order to use them again, I even saw an envelope that had eight labels on top of each other, so that envelope was certainly well used. As I was in the habit of writing to local lads in the forces giving them all the local news, naturally I grabbed any note-paper that I could get. Unfortunately after the war, I disposed of all the letters I received and bitterly regret it now, they would have told a story in themselves.

The hardest to bear was food rationing, particularly when foreign goods became either scarce or unavailable, such as bananas, oranges, Spanish onions, tinned salmon, tinned South African fruit and other such luxuries.

To give you some idea of the quantities we were allowed, I am listing overleaf the amounts we were allocated.

WEEKLY FOOD RATION FOR AN ADULT.

Bacon and ham.	4 ozs.
Meat	To the value of ls.2d. (Metric value 6p approx.) Sausages were not rationed, but were difficult to obtain. Offal was originally unrationed but sometimes formed part of the meat ration.
Butter.	2 ozs.
Cheese.	2 ozs. — Sometimes it rose to 4 ozs. and even up to 8 ozs.
Margarine.	4 ozs.
Cooking fat.	4 ozs. — often dropping to 2 ozs.
Milk.	3 pints — sometimes dropping to 2 pints. Household (skimmed, dried) Was available about 1 packet every 4 weeks.
Sugar.	8 ozs.
Preserves — Jam.	1 lb.
Tea.	2 ozs.
Eggs.	1 real egg a week if available, But at times dropping to 1 every two weeks.
Dried egg.	1 packet every 4 weeks.
Sweets.	12 ozs. every 4 weeks.

In addition, there was a monthly points system:
16 points allowed you to buy one can of fish or meat or 2 lbs of dried fruit or 8 lbs of split peas.

Babies and younger children, expectant and nursing mothers, had concentrated orange juice and cod liver oil from Welfare Clinics together with "Priority Milk". This milk was also available to invalids.

Recipes making full and creative use of the weekly ration were published regularly by the Ministry of Food: "FOOD FACTS" in newspapers and magazines; the B.B.C. also Broadcast useful information on the morning radio programme "Kitchen Front".

As far as sweets were concerned, what my mother did was to combine Dad's, Pam's, mine and her own ration together and then once a month she would purchase the whole amount and then dole out so many sweets per week to each of us and then there could be no arguing. Heaven knows what today's children would make of sweet rationing.

It was amazing the way we 'made do'. English grown fruit was plentiful during their season, so plums, cherries, greengages, pears etc., were bottled for use when out of season. If you had enough sugar, then jam was made and kidney beans were set in rock salt in jars. Anything that could be preserved in any way was used. Luckily vegetables were never rationed and full use was made of them.

It was surprising what meals were conjured up in order to make the meagre ration of meat go round. If I remember correctly, offal was not on ration, so if you were lucky at your butchers, this could be obtained, or if you were luckier still, you might get a wild rabbit which was not on ration. Fish was not rationed either and I take my hat off to the fishermen who risked their lives to go to sea to bring back their hauls. A very good meal could be made with fish. Because all my family liked cheese, this was grated to make it last, it would replace meat or fish when we had a salad. Recipes were often issued by the Ministry of Food but I must admit we preferred to experiment ourselves, not that I did a lot of baking my mother and sister were the experts in that department. My mother, who worked as a Credit Cheque Agent and had many customers, found that a lot of her customers were running short of sugar. Our own shortage mainly consisted of tea, so quite often she would swap sugar for tea. In those days we all helped each other, when we had more of a product than we used, it would be swapped with someone for a commodity that we needed. A regular sight would be a queue outside a shop, then the word would go round as to what they had in stock and in no time these queues would lengthen until the retailer would run out of stock. Although bread was not rationed during wartime, I remember when I was a junior clerk in an office, one of the senior members would ask me to go and queue for a Harvo loaf, which was a fruit loaf.

Another thing we had to get used to was the 'black out'. This took some doing, particularly on very dark moonless nights. What we did was to leave the premises wherever we were, then stand still until our eyes became accustomed to the dark before we moved. To assist us to differentiate between the pavement and the road, the authorities painted all the kerb edges white and believe me that was very helpful, although, of course, when it snowed this aid became ineffectual, but snow lightened all the surroundings, so basically on these occasions we needed no aid.

Listening to the wireless in the early days was very disheartening with the Nazis occupying one country after another. Always my reaction was sadness and to pray that the people of that particular country would be able to bear up under the occupation. However, my reaction was rather different when Norway was occupied. Somehow and there is no explanation for it, I have always felt an affinity with Norway and when they were occupied I cried and cried. I have, in recent years, visited Norway partly to try to discover why I feel so close to that country and partly to see its gaunt, but beautiful scenery. I still do not know why I feel the way I do, perhaps, who knows? It may lie in ancestry because my father hailed from Durham where the Vikings landed on the North East coast close by.

Meanwhile, until 1941, I was still attending school where there was little difference in the general day-to-day life. The air raid shelters for the school were a little distance from the actual building. We had to cross over the girls' playground and then descend steps into what was commonly referred to as 'the shrubbery' where shelters had been erected. We hated going into the shelter (thankfully it was not often) because it was dark and damp and quite frankly, although it was reinforced, I doubt whether it would have survived a direct or even close hit by a bomb.

When clothes rationing came into force, the school authorities had to relax their ruling on school uniform. The main beneficiaries of this rule were new entrants because they did not have to obtain any uniform at all. My uniform lasted me right through school especially as I did not appear to increase in height at all. The only time that I was unable to conform was during the summer when I wore no socks because they took up precious coupons. Clothes were continually changing hands as they were outgrown. A little later after leaving school I became the recipient of many 'hand downs', some of which I was thrilled to have, but others I hated.

Basically, air raids did not dominate life around here until 1940 when the Luftwaffe decided the Midlands was a suitable target. Living only nine miles from the Birmingham area and six miles from the Wolverhampton area, we became accustomed to the wail of the siren, warning us of approaching air raids. At first, we obeyed almost to the letter, to take shelter, but I must admit that eventually the feeling was 'Oh well, if I'm to be a victim let it happen where I am rather than in an uncomfortable shelter'. It was quite easy to recognize the slow and steady drone of the bombers and gradually it seemed that Dudley (where I live) was the point that the bombers used to turn about and take a straight run in to bomb the Birmingham area. This happened so regularly that I am now certain that this was so. I have often wondered if they took their bearings by using our ancient Castle, which stands out, and also 'Top Church' which has a spire that is easily recognizable even from miles away.

In November 1940, there was an horrific concentrated bombing on Coventry that resulted in the first fatal casualty of our local Fire Brigade. Mr. Rogers who was a local hairdresser, was a member of the Dudley Fire Brigade, which responded to the call for more Brigades to attend the Coventry bombing, was killed. He was a respected member of the community and the town mourned his death. I remember going with one of my cousins to see Coventry not long after the bombing and to see the Cathedral with all the rubble around it, with only the shell of the building remaining, really upset me and left a deep impression on me which still affects me. Although the new Cathedral now exists in Coventry alongside the shell of the old one, when I visit there I feel more reverence in the remains of the old Cathedral than in the new one.

Birmingham suffered many raids and I saw quite a lot of the damage caused and goodness knows how many lives were lost. I never saw London and its damage although I have been told that it was on a much greater scale than Birmingham.

Dudley, in a way, came through the bombing very lightly really. In the Oakham/Tividale area a landmine was dropped which caused extensive damage and there was loss of life although I cannot remember the figures. We believe that the target was intended to be 'Big Bertha' a gun emplacement situated quite close by which we often heard booming out trying to bring down enemy aircraft. Whether they ever succeeded I have no knowledge. One night whilst sleeping in our cellar, I was awakened by a big bang. At the time I thought it was 'Big Bertha' but my father, who was a fire watcher during the night on the roof of 'Peacocks', a large store, informed us when he returned in the morning, that a bomb had been dropped by 'Top Church' and that all roads had been closed so there would be no school that day. I needed no second telling and was pleased to stay at home, but on reflection since, I am doubtful if the closed roads extended as far as my school. One remark by a neighbour upon learning of the bombing was that she knew it must have been a bomb because it nearly shook her out of bed! Considering that this lady was well endowed and that I had only thought it was 'Big Bertha' and that this lady slept down her cellar too, I feel there must have been some exaggeration there. The bomb actually fell on a public house opposite the church but luckily the occupants were with the manager and his family at the cinema next door. The public house was gutted, but there was also a lot of damage to the church, particularly the beautiful altar window, which was an unusual one. Shrapnel chipped pieces of the stonework over a wide area of the church and also to the Cooperative Emporium on the opposite side of the street. Naturally windows in the area suffered greatly. Bombs also fell at the rear of the 'Workhouse' that must have looked like a factory from the air, again little damage was done. The only other bombing that I can remember in Dudley occurred whilst I was staying with relatives in Warwick. My uncle, who worked on the railway, came off night duty and said that he had heard that Dudley had been bombed during the night; you can imagine how I felt. Unlike today, when you can pick up the 'phone to find out if everyone are fine, I had to wait until my mother found some way of letting me know they were all O.K. Apparently a factory in Pear Tree Lane had caught fire and by chance enemy aircraft passed over the area and took the opportunity to bomb it. If my memory serves me right, I believe that through natural curiosity, a crowd had assembled to watch the fire and the ensuing bombing which resulted in one death. I have remembered yet another instance with regards to bombing in this area, which was rather a tragedy. A Reception for a wedding was being held at 'The Boat Inn' in Tividale when it received a direct hit by a bomb and killed several people attending the Reception

There was another occasion when Dudley was 'bombed' which caused me to feel a little apprehensive, but also caused some hilarity. The cat I referred to at the beginning always used to ignore the cellar during raids until this particular evening. The sirens had gone and as we had become so accustomed to raids, we did not go down the cellar but carried on as usual. I suddenly noticed that 'Tibby' was standing on the top step of the cellar and then proceeded to descend. I had heard that cats have a sixth sense where danger is concerned and it was then that I began to feel apprehensive. However, my father who had been standing in the street outside our front door suddenly came in yelling. "They're invading, there are parachutes coming down in the Eve Hill area, quick, Mum, help me to get the bath (a large zinc one) into the street and fill it with water." How he expected a bath full of water to repel any invasion I don't know and later when I thought it over, I had a good laugh. As it turned out, the 'invaders with parachutes' were incendiary bombs and water should never be used on these, sand was what was required.

I can't recall any other incidents in the proximity of Dudley but perhaps those of my generation could recall others.

Obviously we became well acquainted with the sight of navy, khaki and Air Force blue uniforms. Also, sadly, we began to hear of local lads losing their lives whilst on active service. One of the earliest was while I was at school. Our history teacher, Mr. Clarke (Nobby he was affectionately known as to us children), joined the Royal Navy but lost his life at sea when his ship was torpedoed. This was a sad loss because he had been a very popular teacher. The only other teacher who did not return (at least to my knowledge) was Mr. Smith, (the professor we called him because his whole appearance fitted the title). Miss Wilson, our geography teacher told me in later years, when I met her in the street, that he had been attached to Intelligence, parachuted into Yugoslavia, but was never heard of again. How true this was I have never been able to discover. There were many names of killed or missing in action that were familiar to me, but only one whom I knew well because I had played with him, his sister and brother when we were younger. This was Jackie Kendall and I had only had a conversation with him a few weeks before he was killed. He was a member of the Parachute Regiment.

I left school in September 1941. Actually it was the second Anniversary of the outbreak of war. I went to work in a solicitor's office as Junior Clerk and remained there until after the end of the war.

Not too long after I started work, one morning the boss came into the office and told us all to get our coats on and go down to the cricket field. When we asked, 'why?' he told us that he had been told that the King and Queen were visiting Dudley but that it had to be kept secret. We duly made our way to the cricket field where to our amazement there were crowds there, mostly school children. So much for it being secret! The King and Queen arrived and they came out on to the balcony of the pavilion so that we could all see them. It certainly gave us all a boost.

When I was fifteen years old, I joined the Girls Training Corp in the hope that later I could enlist in the W.R.N.S., which sadly never materialized, principally because my parents would not sign the consent form, which was needed before I was eighteen. I thoroughly enjoyed my time with the G.T.C. and was trained in marching drill, aircraft recognition, map reading and other areas in preparation for joining the forces. All parades that were held in the town, we were invited to take part. I always enjoyed these, although on the 'Wings for Victory' parade, which was held on a particularly hot day, I nearly passed out. We had been lined up in Netherton for quite some time, standing in the hot sun, when I felt faint. I told my sergeant who was close by and she took me across the road in the shade where I sat on someone's doorstep. The lady living there was watching the parade and she brought me a glass of water and after a little while I was able to rejoin the parade. We marched all the way from Netherton into Dudley, down Castle Hill to the sports ground where we were dismissed. By this time my face was a brilliant red and my fingers had swollen because of the heat.

I remember one 'Red Letter Evening' with the G.T.C. We were going to be inspected by the Area Commandant of the W.A.A.F.'s and other members of her entourage. Our Commanding Officer, Commandant E. Marianne Parry decided to arrange a meal at the Station Hotel for them, but also wanted to include two N.C.O's and two 'other ranks' (Cadets) from our Company. The two Cadets were to be chosen by nominations and votes by the Company. I was lucky to be one of those chosen and if my memory serves me right, Margaret (whom I nicknamed 'Pixie' because she was so petite and had an elfin-like face) was the other Cadet chosen. This was, for me, a very big occasion as I had never been to an hotel for a seven course meal. I looked up everything I could with regards to etiquette, which piece of cutlery to pick up, when to stand and when to sit, when and when not to salute, when and when not to speak. I had to have permission to leave work early to give me time to get home and change into uniform. Although I was overawed by the occasion, I still managed to enjoy it and the meal. Later, after the inspection, the W.A.A.F. Area Commandant complimented the Company on their turn out.

I still have in my possession the shoulder flashes of the Girls Training Corps, 461, Dudley. Also the G.T.C. Service Edition book, two certificates acknowledging that I had passed the required standard for promotion to N.C.O., a one striper known as Assistant Section Leader and the Local Knowledge Test. There is also a newspaper cutting headed 'Colours for Dudley G.T.C.' describing the dedication and presentation of colours, and that the salute was taken by General Sir George Weir. My one regret is that I did not have a photograph taken of me in uniform, but somewhere among my collection of photos, I have a head and shoulders photo of Josie Rudd in uniform.

When I was about seventeen years old, the G.T.C. decided to devote one of their two evening meetings to social events. Originally we were supposed to invite the Sea Cadets, A.T.C. and Army Cadets, but the girls' opinion was that they were only boys and too young! I think it was forgotten that we were only girls! As I had made the acquaintance of several members of the R.A.F. Air Crew Cadets who were receiving training at our local Technical College, many of whom were miles away from home, the decision was made that I should pass on an invitation to them. The response was tremendous, so a rendezvous was selected and as I appeared to be the only one who knew some of them, I had several Cadets with me and as the lads arrived, each Cadet would escort a party to the High School where our meetings were held, until the last one arrived. I think the greatest attraction for the R.A.F. lads was the fact that refreshments were to be provided. We all gave whatever refreshments we could manage to beg from home that proved to be quite a feast for the lads, especially as everything was free for them.

These social evenings were continued for quite a while and as each set of lads were posted elsewhere, they left information behind to let the next set of lads know. Many friendships were formed, but I only know of one that led to marriage and that was one of our Junior Officers.

Meanwhile, the war continued with its mixture of good news and bad. Air raids lessened and were taken over by the 'Doodlebug' and 'Buzz bomb' (the V1 and V2) which were pilotless bombs. These had a limited range and it was the south of the country that suffered. The V1 and V2 must have been horrifying for those who were in their path, because they could be seen and heard, but as soon as the sound ceased, it would plummet down to earth causing havoc and destruction.

I remember an aunt of mine who lived in Kent showing the scars on her body that was the result of a bomb being dropped in her garden, missing its target of the railway line which ran across the bottom of her garden, while she was making gravy in her kitchen. The injuries she received were due to flying glass that scarred her body and looked like veins on the leaf of a tree.

In those days, living in the Midlands, we had never experienced television; we relied principally upon the 'wireless'. Special programmes were created during this time such as 'Music While You Work', 'Worker's Playtime, 'Forces Favourites' and such like. These programmes were relayed throughout factories and places of work and it was found that music was particularly popular because everyone could sing along with it and it helped to keep up morale. 'Worker's Playtime' was broadcast during the workers' lunch time and consisted not only of music but also comedy and any other form of entertainment suitable to the wireless. 'Forces Favourites' was mainly a choice of music from the forces themselves or their families and many 'link-ups' were made between them. Vera Lynn (now Dame Vera Lynn) became highly popular through this programme and was known as 'The Forces Sweetheart'. If my memory serves me right, I believe that Petula Clark, when a little girl, broadcast a message to her father who was serving in India.

My father was involved in the musical side of entertainment provided. He was a member of Harry Pelt's Orchestra from the Dudley Hippodrome and regularly broadcast in 'Music While You Work' and 'Worker's Playtime'. This often involved my mother having to get up extremely early to assist my father to transport his instruments by rail to arrive in time for early broadcasts. It later enabled him to qualify for petrol ration to run a car. I well remember accompanying him to Warley Odeon for a Sunday night concert, during which, at 9 o'clock, the concert was interrupted for a relayed broadcast of one of Winston Churchill's famous speeches. No matter what bad press has been given to Winston Churchill in later years, at that time he epitomized the true Bull Dog British spirit and certainly gave encouragement and heart to us all during the bad times of the war. He never glossed over what we could expect, e.g., 'blood, sweat, toil and tears', but he always held up the light at the end of the dark tunnel, in other words, that we would succeed.

Talking of Dudley Hippodrome brings back memories of many good shows that took place despite the threat of air raids. Tommy Handley came with his show 'I.T.M.A.' (Its That Man Again) and I was very privileged to meet him and Jack Train (a man of many voices), also Sonny Jenks and Rene Williams. One show that I saw was 'Skirts', an all male cast of American servicemen, in fact I still have the sheet music of the title song. It was put over extremely well with many of the men taking very good female parts.

Half way through the war, America entered the fray after Germany declared a state of war between the two countries. We were then 'invaded' by the 'Yanks' which did not go down too well with the lads of our own forces, in fact the phrase used by them was that the Americans were 'over paid, over sexed and over here'. Whether that phrase was used during the First World War or was coined in the Second World War, I do not know. I'm afraid I can't write a lot about the Americans because I never went out with one. This was due to my mother telling me she would kill me if she saw me with one. However, despite my mother's threat, I did meet one American who was extremely pleasant and courteous. The reason that I liked him was the fact that when he asked me to go out with him, I gave all the usual excuses that I was unable to do so, but he must have felt that there was more to it and asked me to give him the real reason. When I told him the truth that my mother had threatened me, he asked if he could accompany me home so that he could ask her direct if he could take me out, but I refused. I must admit that I was very impressed by his request instead of probably laughing at me or being derisory. His name was Howard Fremyan and later on I did, with a friend, arrange to meet him and his pal, but unfortunately my friend and I were late in arriving at the meeting place so I assumed that they had got fed up with waiting and had gone elsewhere. My friend decided to go to their base and if unable to see the lads, she was going to leave our apologies. She related to me the next day, that when she got there, the sentry on duty told her that all the men had been confined to base. Within twenty-four hours the base was deserted. We learned why later, they had gone to assemble in readiness for 'D Day'. Howard was in Company 'C' and I later learned that this particular Company was nearly wiped out during the landings in Normandy. I often think about Howard and hope that he was one of the survivors, but I will never know.

In early 1945 I went into Wolverhampton with a friend shopping and eventually we decided to sit on a seat in the grounds of the church in the main centre of the town to rest our feet. Two airmen joined us on the seat and we noticed the flashes on their shoulders read 'Nederlands' so we asked them how long they had been in England. Unfortunately their knowledge of our language was very limited, but we did manage to glean that their country had been liberated only six weeks previously and they had immediately volunteered for the Dutch Royal Air Force. They were so pleased to be in England and were eager to know all about the local buildings, so we explained those that we knew. It was a pity that the town was Wolverhampton instead of Dudley because we could have provided much more information about our local habitat. I admired these young men because they had wasted no time in volunteering to join the forces in the fight against Nazism.

The war continued with the Allies pressing forward into Europe, liberating large areas, but here, apart from rationing and shortages, we enjoyed life, the days of air raids were over when we lived only for the moment, not knowing whether we would be alive the next day. I went dancing regularly and also went to the cinema, in fact, all the things a teenager wanted to do and was marred only by news of casualties.

Late in the evening on the 7th May, I was at home with the family when we became conscious of singing and laughter in the street. We went to the front door and there were crowds of people coming down the street who informed us that the war was over, at least they said it would be announced the next day. Where they had their information from I do not know, but true enough, on the 8 May 1945, Winston Churchill announced that Germany had surrendered and this day became known as V.E. Day (Victory in Europe). Celebrations were held; everyone decorated their houses and in no time at all everywhere became a mass of red, white and blue. Parades were held, street parties were organized with food appearing like magic, I think everyone had stored up their food in anticipation of victory. Services were held in churches and these made us stop and think about all those who had given their lives in the fight for democracy because it was not only the fighting forces that lost life but also many more were civilians.

As the weeks went on, reports started coming through about concentration camps discovered all round Europe. There were horrifying pictures in the papers that made my stomach turn at the atrocities that were committed by the Nazis. The principal sufferers were the Jews, Gypsies and, in fact, anyone who did not fit into the picture of a perfect Aryan country which Hitler was striving to achieve. How the Allied soldiers coped with these discoveries I do not know, I should imagine it affected their lives forever. It was even worse to see the newsreels at the cinema where you could see everything in detail. The fact that there were survivors was a miracle and it made me realize how lucky I had been to be here never having even joined the lines of refugees, let alone been imprisoned in the concentration camps, or lived under the occupation.

Although the war in Europe had been won, we did not forget the forces in the Far East who were valiantly fighting the Japanese. Victory here was only achieved early by the use of a terrible weapon - the atom bomb. Two were dropped, one on Nagasaki and the other on Hiroshima. The destruction and aftermath of these bombs shocked the world and although it caused the Japanese to surrender which probably saved thousands of Allied forces lives, it has left the world in dread that these weapons should ever be used again. The 15th August 1945 was referred to as V. J. Day (Victory in Japan) but celebrations for this day were rather muted in comparison to V. E. Day, possibly due to the atom bombs. The end of this war even produced horrific details of the atrocities committed by the Japanese, principally in prison camps. There were reports and pictures of starvation and torture of our prisoners of war, also reports of the same to the native people whose countries were occupied and even mass rape of women. What horrors war can reveal.

Obviously, as I said in the beginning, I could only touch on incidents that affected me, greatly or otherwise. Having spent quite some time in writing what I have, I can appreciate any book that I read now, because it is tough going to string words together to make some meaning and how authors can write book after book I really don't know, it must be a gift.

Before I end, I should like to make one further point. Some years after the end of the war, I read a book entitled 'Thine Enemy' by Sir Philip Gibb, where he recounts personal experiences by German people, made into a story. That book had a profound effect on me and made me realize that there are always two sides to a story. The sufferings of some of the ordinary German people were also horrific, both from the Nazis and from Allied bombardment. There were horrific atrocities committed by Russians as they advanced through Germany. I always used to say during the war that we were fighting the Nazis because even then I assumed that there were Germans who did not want to fight and only wanted peace. Dictatorship does not always mean that only opponents in other countries suffer, but also their own people who do not agree with the regime. Unfortunately the end of the Second World War has not meant the end of any war, because wars are still being fought today throughout the world. I'm afraid my dream of a world at peace will never be attained, certainly not in my lifetime, but oh, if only it could be achieved, the world would then be a real Utopia. Unfortunately as long as greed and power exist, a dream like mine will only remain a dream.

To my children and grandchildren, my hope is that there will never be a Third World War, because war is not the glamourised picture that the television and cinema would have you believe, it is soul destroying and prolifically evident by vacant places at the table replaced only by gravestones and people maimed and injured either physically or mentally. I was a lucky person during the war, I lived life almost normally and managed to have fun and enjoyment, but I would never wish those times returned. My prayer for you all is for eternal Peace.

Sylvia Thomas

RECOLLECTION OF THE WAR YEARS

Looking through a pile of old photographs the other day, I came across a couple that were taken in the early part of the last World War, that is 1939 - 1945. As I looked at it memories of those War years flashed in front of me, for in the photo was myself and a group of workmates standing in the yard where we were on our lunch break, outside the press shop of Elkingtons and Company Ltd. We were all smiling and I wondered what those workmates were doing now and where they all lived. It would be nice I thought to write about those times during the War.

That fateful day in 1939, Sunday the third of September, when Neville Chamberlain's words came over the radio in very grave tones, "we are now at War with Germany," so many lives were to change. I was nearing my sixteenth birthday, in fact to be precise, I would be sixteen in eight days time on the eleventh day of September 1939.

I had left school at the age of fourteen had a job in a Steam Laundry at Blackheath where I lived, but only stayed one week. Then I got a job at a jewelry manufactures in Soho and Winson Green where I was comfortably settled in a nice clean job as a jewelry setter. It was interesting work and I loved it; and now I had got to leave to go into munitions. I thought, as so many did, and I said to my mother, "It wont be for long Mom and I can get my old job back again". How wrong we all were.

My father, who was a skilled tool turner worked for Elkingtons and Company in Newhall Street Birmingham, which was a well known name in Cutlery and Holloware, and they too turned part of there factory over to the making of munitions during the War period. I was able to get a job there and travelled to work with my father. My brother also worked there as a maintenance worker, which made my mother happy to know that we were all together.

My sister Stella worked close to home at T.W. Lench of Blackheath who manufactured nuts and bolts and was only a few minutes away from our house which was 59 Mackmillan Road, Blackheath, near Birmingham.

My first job I remember was working on an hand press clipping the fraze off wing nuts, that had been hot forged in the stamping department. I soon get into the swing of it and was turning out a good quota each day. To stop us getting bored we moved around each day on a different press and I also worked a power press, blanking out parts for the bayonet scabbard, then forming them on another power press. The work was so different from delicate jewelry setting and my hands were soon rough and cut. Meanwhile everyone was frantically making blackout curtains for windows and doors ready for the dark nights that were to come. Identity cards were issued and food rationing began with a Ration Book for each member of the family. Anderson Shelters were delivered to every home and we set about digging out a place in the garden to erect it. I think we used ours about half a dozen times then it filled up with water. Gas Masks were next issued and we had to carry them everywhere we went, and it became automatic to pick it up when you went out.

Clothing coupons and Sweet Coupons came on the scene and queues for everything from cigarettes to groceries formed. You just got in them, then asked what it was for.

I remember the first air raid, it was most frightening, the wailing sirens woke us from our sleep, and we all just fled down the shelters. We would hear the planes overhead and wondered where they were heading. Then the All Clear sirens would go and we would all go back to bed. After going through that a time or two we stayed in bed for it was very cold in those shelters. Lord Haw-Haw, whom the Germans used to spout propaganda on the Radio, would name well known factories in and around our area that they were going to blow to bits tried to make us believe our number was up. We were very lucky in Blackheath for no real damage was done, but in and around Birmingham it was a different story.

One woman I worked with was bombed out three times, she would come to work the morning after being in the public shelters all night to tell us all, "Well girls, Jerry's bleeding well done it again," her home no longer there. She never let it get her down, and none of her family were ever hurt. Going to work one morning after a heavy raid the night before, I remember as the train pulled into Snow Hill Station, the platforms were all littered with broken glass that had shattered from the canopies above, and some of it was still dangerously hanging so we all were directed another way out to avoid being cut, for as more trains thundered in the vibration was causing more glass to fall. I believe that was the night a bomb hit our work and caused a corner of it to be badly damaged. My brother was on fire watch duty that night, and he said he would never forget it.

I was then moved to another department to work on the Bren Gun Platform. There were quite a number of operations on this small part for the Bren Gun. I was the first operation on a milling machine. My work was then passed along to the second operation and then on to the third and so on all down the line to the last. We worked as a team and pooled the money, so that we all got the same as each other. 1000 we turned out complete each day, and we helped each other as our quota was finished, so that by the time it was time to go home we were all cleaned up and the milling machines ready for the next day.

After a week or two on this job, we needed a bigger output, so a night shift was introduced with another team of workers, and this meant I had to work two weeks days and two weeks nights. The hours were much longer on the night shift but we doubled our output to 1000 finished day and night. It was tedious work and my stomach suffered, for just as I got used to eating at night, I was on days and vice versa, and I never seemed to get enough sleep. The night shift hours were 8 o'clock at night to 7 o'clock next morning, and the days were 8 o'clock to 6 o'clock

Travelling in the blackout was another nightmare. The railway carriages would be in almost darkness and with the blinds drawn we would never know if we were at the right station and we would listen for the guard to shout out the name of the station we had pulled in. The streets also were totally black, no street lamps to light the way. The windows of all the houses all blacked out, not daring to show the slightest chink of light for fear of letting Jerry see it.

About two miles from our house a great naval gun was installed which we nick-named Big Bertha. It was on top of Turners Hill and by golly when it was in action it shook the houses around, even ours and we were quite a distance away. Also, barrage balloons were dotted here and there.

Life went on just the same, I think the British people easily adapt to change very quickly, and even enjoy a joke about it. No wonder we are called the Bulldog Breed.

Clothing Coupons really hit us hard. I remember buying a great army blanket, I believe it was grey or maybe khaki, anyway I had it dyed Navy Blue, and then had it made up into a winter coat. It wore like iron and was lovely and warm, I think we tried every trick there was for clothes when our coupons had been all used up. The one hundred weight sugar bags we would get from the grocers, we boiled till they were white and then hemmed round and embroidered for use as tablecloths, also the muslin from around the lamb carcasses we boiled till clean and white to make us full things for the home.

Our diet wasn't rich either, the bread was neither white nor brown, it must have had all the vitamins though for we all appeared to be healthy. Fruit also was scarce, by fruit I mean imported fruit such as peaches and oranges and bananas, for children born just before the War and after grew up not knowing what a banana was, and oranges were on ration books for children only.

Fashion in clothes and hairstyles I think were good. Lots of knitted fair isle jumpers and pullovers were worn and the puffed sleeve that is so fashionable now were very popular. Shoes had more style I think than they do now and were made much better. Hairstyles, well sweeps were in and well I remember the Snoods we wore to hold our long hair in place. Turbans also were very prominent in the working girls' wardrobe. They looked smart and hid the curlers while at work. Silk stockings were scarce, so the alternative was to colour our legs and draw a line down the back for the seam.

Food was the biggest problem, my mother would rack her brains for ideas to make our dinners more interesting for the meat ration was almost nil, and my father was a fussy eater. We used to get a food parcel now and again from my fathers brother in Canada, and we would shout for joy at the tins of bacon that were in it and mother would say, "Well folks a treat today for tea, bacon and eggs." When we get eggs they were kept in a bucket of issinglass to keep them fresh. Also there was the dried egg we could buy. It resembled a great big omlette when cooked all puffed up, then it just simply went flat, but still, we got to like it and wasn't too bad at all. I've often wondered what happened to it as there is so much dried food today it would be very handy.

At work we were all grafting, turning out more and more munitions, but the shift work played havoc with my social life. I loved roller skating and dancing and the weeks I was on days wasn't too bad, but the night shift was another matter, still we all had to make sacrifices one way or another. Slogans were put up like, "be like dad and keep mum," and "careless talk can cost lives", and "give us the tools and we will finish the job". Winston Churchill would be on the radio giving us pep talks to keep up our morale.

In the cinema we watched film stars like James Cagney, Humphry Bogart, Clark Gable, Edward G. Robinson, Betty Grable, Alice Faye, Sonja Henie. Gangster and Musicals were most popular, with Westerns thrown in for good measure. We had three picture houses in Blackheath with the Odeon in Long Lane not far away. The skating rink in Ross near home was open five times a week and I spent a lot of my leisure hours there, that is until early 1940 when it caught fire and burned down to the ground and was sadly missed by a lot of people. Also it was never re-built. I went to local dances with a girlfriend and we had many happy times together.

Meanwhile Lord Haw-Haw still spouted the propaganda on the Radio. I seem to remember he was an Englishman working for the Germans. Coventry had a real thumping. In fact I don't think they had many nights free from the bombing raids.

My mother's brother Frank lived at Quarry Bank which is about three miles from Blackheath. He lived in house which was situated at the back of a cobblers shop in the High Street. You had to go up a long entry, then a passage way, and there right at the back stood two houses back to back. Uncle Frank lived in one with his wife and mother in law, and in the other one lived his wife's sister and her husband. There was only gas in the houses and I don't think: many people knew that the houses were there, and the postman relied on there address reading 'Back of Thompson's Cobblers

Shop.' The school higher up the High Street made it that the playground railings backed onto these two houses. It was my uncle's practice to fetch his evening paper after tea. This particular night, it was Friday and dark. With his torch he made his way down to the little low gate, down the passage into the entry and out onto the street. The paper shop was only a little way down, got his paper and on the return up the entry, along the passage to his gate. As he went to open the gate, something puffed in his face. He stood still and shouted, "Who's there," got no answer. He tried. to open the gate and this thing puffed in his face again, he shone his torch and there hanging from an outbuilding was a parachute. Uncle Frank just froze, he thought there was a German there. He looked up again and saw to his horror it was a land mine swinging like a great big dustbin almost to the ground. He said he never knew how he get passed it but when he got in the house my aunt could see by his face that something was wrong and said "what is it Frank?" He quickly told her and said. "Nell get your mother out and down the entry as fast as you can and I'll go and tell Annie and Walter next door." They all managed to get down the entry and went to relatives and uncle Frank rang the police station and told them what was hanging in his garden. Quarry Bank was evacuated that night. The bomb disposal squad came quickly and took out the detonator. Two land mines came down that night, the other one was on the school not far away from the other. I don't think I will ever forget uncles face as he told us of this experience. I remember him saying to my mother, "Liz," he said, my mothers name was Elizabeth, I aged ten years in those few moments, for if they had gone off, Quarry Bank would have been wiped out. A special service was held in chapels and churches that Sunday night, and as one preacher put it in his prayer, "God had walked through Quarry Bank" that weekend.

 My pay packet at work was very good for working in a team paid dividends, and I saw to it that my mother shared in my good wage. Both my sister and I now paid 'board' at home and as I had a better paid job than she did, I was able to give mother more money, and also after work on Saturdays I would go down the Bull Ring and buy her some goodies. It was the old Bull Ring then with all the barrow boy sellers and the old Fish Market, a thriving place just packed out with shoppers getting in their weekend shopping. I would get a rabbit and a crab and I remember one time I bought my mother a lovely big peach, it cost the earth, for even in War time if you had the money you could buy almost anything. Anyway it was worth every penny to see her face as she tucked into it with the juice running down her chin, for she loved fruit. I would buy some gingerbread snaps that weren't on ration too. The Bull Ring always seemed to have more choice of available foods than at Blackheath and I think it's the same today.

We had our Home Guard at Elkingtons made up from the men who worked there, and I remember that very sad occasion one night shift I was at work. It would be about ten o'clock and we were on a tea-break and the Home Guard were making their rounds around the work checking everything was alright. Our department was on the second floor of the new building with a fire escape. About five of them came in through the fire escape that night and had a chat with our foreman whom we called Chalky because his surname was White, then they wished us all goodnight and went down to the air-raid shelters where they had their quarters. As they went down the steps, which were concrete, Johnny the Welsh lad who was only about twenty, fell and hit his head on the steps. His mates all Welsh picked him up and helped him down the shelter. He said how his head hurt and wanted to lie down, so he got onto his bunk for a nap. His mates saw that he was comfortable and left him asleep, and they did his turn on duty. But come morning when they tried to waken him they found that he had died, from the bang on his head which was later found to have bled internally.

It was a vary sad night for Elkingtons and I don't think any of us on that night shift will ever forget him for he was always laughing and joking and he was in our thoughts for a long, long time. They took his body back to his home in Wales for burial, for he was only lodging in Birmingham and had come to work in munitions.

Coming home on the train one morning after a night shift, I had a most frightening experience, and as the train pulled into Hockley Station, the next stop after Snow Hill, I jumped out of the carriage and into another one which was quite full of people. I was still trembling when I got home and my mother could see by my face that something was the matter. When I told her about this man who was in the railway carriage, she said, "that's it, you aren't working anymore nights till you have someone to travel home with." There wasn't anyone who lived our way so I asked if I could do permanent days. The answer was no, so I was transferred to another department where I was working days all the time. It was a big drop in pay, but at least I had peace of mind.

I was moved to the side of Elkingtons where my father worked, Newhall Street mill, or press shop. Here they did stamping and press work, hand presses, and power presses, and double action power presses. A double action power press as its name implies, first the punch come down and forms the metal into the bed of the press, then goes up and comes down again and draws the metal through and stretches it and then it falls through into a pan underneath the press. My father made the tools for these presses and many more. He was well liked at work for he was very clever at his job, in fact when the tool setters had any trouble with a press, they would fetch my father to listen to it for they always said of him, 'fetch old Pat, he'll only have to listen and he'll tell you what's wrong.' He was always called Pat, I never heard anyone call him Frank or Mr. Patrick, and he did 45 years service at Elkingtons and retired at 64.

I worked on the hand and power presses for quite a time and then a girl by the name of Betty Ingram and myself were moved again to work on drilling machines on the sten gun magazine. She was a Welsh girl and we became very good friends, and many times she would come home with me at weekends to stay with us for she said she could get a goodnights' sleep. She lived in Handsworth and they got a lot of heavy raids there. I remember one Friday afternoon when we were clearing our drilling machines of swarf and getting ready to go home, Betty bent her head and forgot she had taken off the guard from her driller, her hair at the front above her forehead got caught around the drill, she screamed and I turned round to see what had happened and to my horror her hair was being pulled from her head. I had the sense to press the off button and at the same time I grabbed the pulley belt to try and stop the machine quicker. She was in a terrible state of shock, and after I untangled her hair from the drill I sent for the nurse. Fortunately she hadn't lost too much of her hair but it bled a great deal and that frightened her more. It took quite a while for her hair to grow again but she changed her way of arranging it so that it wasn't seen. I don't think we ever forgot that afternoon, and even now when I hear from her she mentions it.

We worked in this department for the remainder of the War years. They were happy years despite the fact we were at War and all the rationing and blackouts and air-raids that went with it we could still have fun and enjoy ourselves.

The Americans soldiers were being billeted all over England and we had our share of them in the Midlands. Chewing gum and spending money like there was no tomorrow it's little wonder why there were so many G.I. brides. Our girls loved the attention they got from them and all the silk stockings that were going. At the local dances they would swagger in and ask you for a dance, well you couldn't call it dancing, more like shuffling along. I think they had the time of their lives while they were over here.

Two childhood playmates of mine, in fact we had lived on the same yard for eleven years, were called up in the forces, one in the air-force and the other in the army whose names were Dickie Hughes and Joey Wheeler. Sadly they were both killed in action, but I can still remember them both as children when we played so happily on the yard in Darby Street, those happy days I will never forget.

At work things were going just the same, the boss who owned Elkingtons was a Baron, an Austrian by the name of Baron Von-Newrath, a pleasant man who would make his rounds of the factory and stop to talk to you if you happened to meet him. It seemed strange to me that we were making munitions to kill Germans, and here we were working for an Austrian Jew who hated Hitler.

Meanwhile we would listen to Vera Lyn on the radio who by now was called the Forces Sweetheart and whose popular songs such as The White Cliffs of Dover and We'll Meet Again, were being played and recorded and they were selling very well. The records then were the old 78's. My father bought a radiogramme, it was an Alba, and I started to collect the latest records of that time. Bing Crosby, Joe Loss and his band, Deana Durbin, and many, many others.

In Summer we had double Summer Time which meant it was light at night much later and I think it was a very good idea also it was a great help to the farmers and shift workers. In the black out we were never afraid to go out alone, not like today when we are being constantly warned not to venture out alone because it is not safe.

As the year 1945 came in it seemed there was now a light at end of the tunnel, our forces were driving the enemy back rapidly and as the month of May approached it was announced on the radio that the War in Europe would soon be over. And so on the 8th of May 1945 Britain rejoiced and celebrated our victory over Adolf Hitler and his cronies. Then in August the War in Japan was declared over and what a time we had. Parties in the streets with huge bonfires blazing and people sharing what rations they had to put on a spread in the streets, table after table of food and drink especially if any of our lads had come home it was a double celebration. Flags were put up with many Welcome Home signs stretched across the streets I remember going with a friend from one party to the next and it went on till late at night and the singing could be heard everywhere,

As we got back to normal, at work there was to be great change back to peacetime manufacture. Betty Ingram and myself were asked if we would like to learn the silver soldering, We were both keen for we did not want to leave Elkingtons, so we said yes and as a result we were moved to the soldering department and were taught how to solder the metal handles of the knives onto the blade. It was a most interesting job and we both took to it like ducks to water. Our foreman was named Charlie Powell and he was just great to work for and we got on like a house on fire. Altogether there were seven of us doing this work and our output wasn't bad at all.

We were paid £3 5 shillings a week day-rate and we got 3 pence a dozen for all the knives we soldered. When they left our department they were then highly polished and engraved. We had orders for ships like the P and O Lines, restaurants like Lyons and many other notable hotels for they were made to last. I bought some cutlery at cost price while I was there and I still have today and they are as good now as the day I bought them. My father bought me an oval teapot of which he had made the tools to manufacture. He bought it me to commemorate the coronation of Queen Elizabeth in 1953 and I still have it along with a few more pieces of other hollow ware made at Elkingtons and Company.

I stayed there till I got married but my dad remained there till he was 64 when he retired for health reasons having completed 45 years service. They were happy years despite everything and my brother and I often reminisce about those years when half of our family worked together at the same firm Elkingtons and Company Newhall Street Birmingham manufactures of cutlery and hollow ware which is still remembered as one of the very best and is known throughout the world.

Tossie Patrick

THE LONG SHIFT

Just a few stops left, then back to the depot. Nine o'clock he'd make it by. There'd been no breakdown and they were a driver short so Alf had taken the 42 out. He hadn't questioned the request. You didn't, there was a war on. People just did what they could for the common good, like grow your own vegetables, use any scrap of land for the purpose. And that's what Alf would be doing at the weekend. Not a scrap of land for him though, he'd be down on his allotment, tending the vegetable crop. He knocked off at 9.00pm and wasn't on again till 6.00am on Monday. That was a full 57 hours by Alf's reckoning.

At the last stop, the terminus it said on the sign, the last passengers got off. Alf turned the bus around and headed back to the depot.

"Loaded?"
"Loaded!"

It was a saft question. Everyone could see it was loaded, it was big enough, a huge bit of machinery bound for Middlesborough, one of the arms factories. Again, vital, part of the war effort, a Ministry order in effect, and it was loaded onto one of the huge Thornycroft lorries. It was a relief to see it pull slowly out of the works.

It was barely an hour later that a young lad appeared at Ted's office, red faced and out of breath. Flustered he might have been, but the message was clear enough. The Thornycroft had broken down. The gearbox had gone. It happened, especially if some clarnet hadn't topped up the fluid. Somebody would be for the ruddy high jump if that was the case, but no, this couldn't be happening.

Ted borrowed the gaffer's car and went to look for himself, and it was right. There was nothing for it but to change the gear box where the Thornycroft had ground to a halt in Wednesbury. The driver didn't seem too put out. Knew all the answers. Get the repair crew out, work on it over the weekend. It would be ready to roll by Monday. That would free his weekend up. He'd got something on until this job came up, and it wasn't tending his allotment. Might have been put down as tending someone else's allotment though, her mon's away in the army. Ted didn't know anything about the driver's weekend of passion ruined by the call of duty but now back on again, but he did know the repair crew were out on a job taking a rear axle off a lorry over in Coventry. He'd only sent them out an hour before the Thornycroft left the yard. All weekend they'd be on that job. To get a repair team on the Thornycroft, he have to find one first. He couldn't call them off the Coventry job, Ministry contract, essential, just like this one. Ruddy war. Be glad when this lot's over.

Alf pulled into the depot. Either he needed glasses or that was Sid, his oppo from the breakdown truck. Sid, the joker, had a smile on his face. He'd taken another bus out too but his route meant an 8.30 finish. Alf couldn't see what was funny about hanging around until 9.00 for him to finish. Sid would never hang around.

"Knocked off for the wikend Alf?" Sid asked, taking a drag from his Woodbine.

"Ar, working on me allotment."

"That's what yoe think. We'n got a job on."

Alf did a quick inventory of all the buses in the depot. All seemed present and correct, but a few weren't back yet. Joe, the gaffer appeared from the office. What was he still doing here at this time? And who was that bloke he'd got in tow?

Ted explained that their Thornycroft was out of action with a broken gearbox and it needed changing pronto. Ministry job, there's a war on et cetera. Alf didn't need telling there was a ruddy war on. What was comical was the pronto in relation to changing a Thornycroft gearbox. He'd shot Sid a glance at that and Sid had grinned.

Half an hour later, after being conveyed to the scene in Ted's gaffers car, they surveyed the stricken lorry by torchlight.

"Fust thing'll be ter get some lighting set up. We woe be able to do this waving ruddy torches around."

"An it'll have to be covered over less we'll have the ARP after we." Sid observed.

He was right, the blackout was still on meaning there could be no stray light.. Ted had been busy however.

"It's being sorted. Home Guard are bringing an arc light over and rigging up some awning. That should keep the ARP sweet. Don't need them telling us there's a ruddy war on."

On cue, they heard the whine of a Bedford lorry.

"At least summats on time this wikend."

Half an hour later Alf and Sid were alone, left to their gearbox.

"They am ruddy ockard these things."

"They'm alright if yoe'm stood in a pit under em but we shall be here all night getting these ruddy nuts off."

They took it in turns, half an hour each. The ARP Warden showed up at 1.00 am to see what was going on. He came over all officious, inspecting the awning. The Home Guard lads had done a good job cutting out any stray light. Once arrangements had been seen to meet his exacting standards he stopped being an irksome little jobsworth and started being a decent sort of bloke.

"Have to see if I can organise you lads some tea."

And it duly arrived at 1.30.

"Who'n yoe know as brews up at half one in the morning?"

The warden touched the side of his nose with his forefinger and winked.

"Oughta be a law against it," Sid muttered after he'd gone.

Alf appeared from under the lorry. "Sup that tay, then its yower turn.

Being summer, it didn't seem long until they saw the first streaks of light across the sky to herald the dawn. The gaffer showed up at seven and noticed the teacups.

"What yer think this is, the ruddy Ritz?"

"Ar," Alf said, "we thought yoe'd come to deliver we breakfast."

The gaffer glared at Sid who was giving Alf a quizzical look because he'd just come out with the sort of thing he would say.

"Everything's OK then?"

"Ar," Sid said. "The Warden's bit of stuff's seein we'm fixed."

He turned and left. "Well, if he had come ter get we breakust, we shor get none now."

It was after nine when Ted arrived with bacon and eggs. "Sorry I'm late boys but I've had the devil's own job getting hold of these."

'Bacon and egg!' Sid was thinking, 'we'll have to work all night again.'

Ted had been burning the midnight oil too. As well as seeing his rescuers get fed, he had been organising lifting gear and replacement gearbox. The former would arrive mid morning, the latter sometime the following night. When Ted left, they tucked into their breakfast.

"Thought he was never gonna goo, gooin on abaht liftin gear an' gearboxes."

They finished their meal in silence.

"That's gonna sit heavy," Alf said eventually.

"Ar, ah'll be noddin off," Sid agreed.

"Well if we both drap off we'll be away for hours," Alf said.

They'd both been on the go for over 24 hours now.

"Yoe get off for an hour then ah'll wake yer up and we'll tek it in turns for a bit so as we can catch up on a bit of kip."

Sid went and settled himself in the cab as best he could while Alf soldiered on. They managed to get a couple of hours each in that way until the lifting gear arrived early afternoon. It took a couple of hours to set up the crane from the parts delivered. Ted arrived at 5.00 with a load of sandwiches and flasks of tea.

"Here, this lot should keep yer gooin. The game ah've had."

"We've had a game putting that together. Came in bits. It's ready now though. Another four or five hours and we'll put the chains round to tek the weight, then we'll loosen it off completely, swing it round and put the old one down there."

"They'll be here tonight with the new one. Just tell em where ya need things ter go. I've told em that at this site, yoe two am the gaffers."

"Two gaffers and no workers," Sid said under his breath to Alf. "No wonder it's tekin so ruddy long."

It was getting dark again when Sid said, "best got that awning over and that light set up or we'll have that ARP bloke on the warpath. On cue the warden appeared.

"Come to help yoe two set yer light up."

They were finished in half an hour. Ten minutes to set it up again, another twenty to pass inspection.

"Well, at least he came to help," Sid said after warden had gone. The chains were in place now, bearing the weight. "Just get them last nuts undone then swing it round."

"No sign of that new gearbox so we might get some shut eye till they get here."

"Forget that one Alfie boy, this must be it now."

With the help of the men on the lorry they unloaded the new gearbox, loaded the old one, and swung the new one into place. It was four hours before the lorry pulled away. It was the early hours of the morning again when they started fitting the new gearbox.

"We'll sleep in shifts again," Sid suggested. And they did. When it was their turn awake it was becoming difficult to keep going. The flasks were empty and the sandwiches gone.

It was a fine Sunday morning, warm. One of the women from the houses opposite brought some tea over and some bread and scrape. That bucked them up a bit.

"See Alf, yoe wouldn't a wanted to work on the allotment on a day like this, sweatin cobs."

"Yoe'm right there Sid. Much rather be sweatin cobs here with yoe."

Ted put in another appearance late afternoon. The box was almost completely refitted by then. What followed was the putting back of everything they'd had to strip out in the first place to get the damned thing out.

"More fittle lads? Set yer up for the fun part."

It was the fun part. Alf and Sid had never worked on a Thornycroft before. One of their own lorries, Bedfords, they could have done, as the saying goes, in their sleep, which was how they were operating now to all intents and purposes. They had laid everything out on sacking so they'd know what order to put it back in.

"This'd be bad enough if they were wide awake."

"An it would."

It was five o'clock when the last piece was in place.

"E ar then, let's fire it up," sid said. "Ah've always wanted a goo in one o these."

The mighty Thornycroft turned over and roared into life. Sid crunched the new gears but eventually found first then inched forwards. Alf, who'd had a look of terror on his face from the moment Sid suggested firing up, didn't relax until Sid was down by his side again.

"Easy," Sid said.

"It wor the startin ah was worried abaht, it was stopping. Ah could see all that government equipment gooin inter them houses over theer after we'd spent all weekend getting it mobile again."

They tidied up and went back to the depot. The gaffer was there, just got in, with a brew on.

"Any tay in that pot gaffer?"

"Ar there is, an it's all spoke for."

"Charmin. Here, the kays ter the breakdown."

"An where dun ya think yoe two am gooin?"

"Um ter get a wash an some kip."

"Kip! There's drivers short so ah need yoe two aht on the routes."

"But we've on'y just finished that job on the Thornycroft..."

"Wor nuffin ter do wi this depot."

"Come on gaffer."

"Come on nuffin."

"57 hours we'n just put in gaffer," Alf said plainly. So far only Sid had done the protesting.

"Not you an all Alf. Don't you know there's a ruddy war on. Get them buses aht. There's workers gorra be took to factories..."

How they never had accidents that morning, Alf and Sid wondered about right through to senility. At the end of the shift the gaffer called them in.

"Ted's bin round with yer wages for yer weekend foreigner."

They couldn't be paid cash. Alf and Sid took their packets of Players apiece and left in silence. Hard to come by these, there was a ruddy war on.

LOCK OUT

The train had come out of Rowley Regis station right on time, 06.30 a.m., and Irene had been in time for it leaving her home in Rowley Village in good time for the walk down the hill towards Blackheath and on to the station. Getting to the station on time was entirely within her own control. What happened once she got there wasn't. That this morning's train was on time was all well and good. It could get her into Witton with plenty of time to spare to get to the Button. Could and would, just as long as there were no hold ups. There was a war on and there was no guarantee that there'd be no hold ups. Troop trains had priority...

...And that was why Irene's train was stuck at Black Patch. It couldn't go anywhere until the troop train going north out of New Street had passed. Minute passed minute. Five became ten, and then fifteen. There was still time to spare, but that was fast disappearing.

At last the troop train began to pass. It was a long one and it seemed to crawl, but the last coach finally went by leaving clear track. Irene's train still wouldn't be able to go until the signal was clear. More waiting... When the steam finally chuffed intent and the wheels clattered in response, it would be touch and go whether Irene could make it. She would have to run all the way from Witton Station to the factory and still might not make it for 08.00 a.m.. Even a minute past was no good. A miss was as good as a mile as far as the management at the Button was concerned. One minute past 8.00, that was all, just one minute and you were locked out and wouldn't be allowed in until 9.00. A full hour's money lost. It was a common practice, if you were late for work you missed the full hour. It was a big incentive to be on time. Almost all of the workers were women who were brought into industry for the war effort, and as most of them came from the streets of Aston near the factory, it was a practice that was viewed, by and large, as fair enough.

At a distinct disadvantage however were the half dozen or so Black Country girls who made their way to Aston by train. With priority on the railways being given to the military, they could end up late for work irrespective of their own best efforts. If they were late because they had to stop for a en route for a troop train to pass, as they did this morning, then it could hardly be passed off as fair that they would lose an hour's money.

The train pulled into Witton. Even running all the way, it was doubtful. Maybe if she ran faster than she had ever run before, then maybe... And she did, but it was not enough.

It was a pleasant July summer morning when she'd left Rowley. Waiting for the troop train to pass Black Patch, Irene had concluded it was going to be a hot one. But the air was still. Only the night before the talk had been of an impending storm.

The first big spots had fallen as she ran from the station, sporadic at first, the stuff of sun showers that pass after a minute or two if they last that long, or the precursor to a real storm. Some of the most torrential rain Irene had ever experienced had fallen in July. She'd seen it washing in torrents down Rowley Village.

The heavy spots splashed on the ground making dark marks where they fell, one here, another a foot or so there. It went like that all the way along to the gatehouse. The Button was a big factory and as the name would suggest, made buttons. Its contribution to the war effort was to produce the buttons for the uniforms of the armed forces, from admiral to able seaman, air vice marshal to aircrew, colonel to corporal, you name it, the Button made it. It had its own gatehouse, and concierge – Mr Silkin, who had served in the last lot, on the Somme. He knew all about discipline and following orders. At 8.00 sharp, he shut the gates. It was a lock out, with Irene on the wrong side, catching her breath, watching the dark patches on the ground getting smaller in diameter but closer and closer together. Then all of a sudden, like turning on a shower, the deluge started. It was as bad as anything she'd seen that had caused Rowley Village to run like a river.

There were a few local girls outside the gate and they quickly scurried home to the shelter of their own homes. Irene looked around and nothing became immediately obvious as a source of shelter other than the gatehouse itself. She tried to attract the attention of the concierge, "Mr Silkin, sir, can I shelter in there please sir."

He shook his head. It wasn't out of badness, it just wasn't within his authority to permit it, and his years in the British Army had taught him the wisdom of not allowing anything that was not within your authority to permit. It could get you ruddy shot!

Irene looked around with some sense of urgency. She was already drenched and there was no sign that the rain was easing up. It had gone dark, it was more like a grey November afternoon than a July morning. She ran to the other side of the road and tried to shelter as best she could in a doorway though in reality it offered precious little by way of protection and she couldn't have been any wetter than she was already.

Just before 9.00 the gates opened and she was allowed in along with the other Black Country who had similarly sort shelter and who had been similarly unsuccessful. The few Brummies who had been late came scurrying from their houses having given themselves just enough time to get through the gate before it shut again at 9.00.

The lock out was particularly unfair to the Black Country girls but this morning's events made it seem downright iniquitous. It wasn't a case of "I don't know what possessed me," this was a case of if something's not right then you should say so. And Irene did.

"It's not fair, Mr Silkin," she advised the concierge. "There's a war on. Us Black Country girls can't help it if a troop train holds us up like it did this morning. If the company can't change the lock out they could at least let us shelter in the gatehouse in the bad weather until we can get in to work."

The exchange was over with Irene off to her bench without Mr Silkin having contributed to it or indeed having chance to contribute to it. It was just as well the mood Irene was in, she wouldn't have put up with a "there's nothing I can do about it." And in essence it was true, Mr Silkin didn't make the rules, he upheld them. He couldn't therefore change the rules, so "there's nothing I can do," was never uttered. Nor would it have been because strictly speaking it wasn't true, there was something he could do. He could advise those who did make the rules of a little unfairness.

It was the following week that Irene was called into the office.

The summoning made heads turn. Knowing nods and glances were exchanged, as well as those lips pursed in agreement. There was only one reason for being called to the office so there was nothing really to disagree about. Cards. Irene was going to get her cards. It could only be because she had torn Mr Silkin off a strip the morning of the rains. That was the story that had become established as the facts of the matter at any rate.

For his part, Mr Silkin knew the facts of the matter, and what he had said to those who make the rules he upheld. He knew that Irene had been called to the office and that calls to the office meant one thing and one thing only: cards. He hoped that the young woman didn't get the sack on what would in effect be on his account. That certainly hadn't been his intention, but he couldn't see any other outcome. Rules is rules, even unwritten ones.

Irene wasn't fearful, even though she knew what was coming. No one would ever be able to convince her that either the lock out or the withholding of shelter were right. And they didn't. It was almost with a smile that the big boss said that in the bad weather her was instructing Mr Silkin to allow the Black Country girls to shelter in the gatehouse... if they were late and it was a lock out.

THE EVACUEES

I was born in 1930 in Wilnecote (pronounced Wincote by the locals back then) a few miles from Tamworth. Nowadays it is part of the town's urban sprawl but before the war it was very much a separate village. A little village in which everyone knew everyone else, and everyone knew everyone else's business. It was, as you'd expect, a rural community, there were farms all around but in fact most of the men worked down the mines, so you could say there was a mix of agriculture and industry. We had an influx of Bevin Boys to work in the mines in the war. My granddad had worked down the mines when he was young but he had an accident, bursting his knee. He went and worked at Doultons the pottery people after that. In 1935 my parents bought a house for £450. It was on Overwoods Road. The adjoining Jonkel Avenue was named after John Kelly, the builder who put the houses up. Fields rolled into the distance from our house. We used to play in a big field between the back of our house and Jonkel Avenue. It was land owned by a brewery earmarked for a pub that was never built. We used to dig holes over there and put tents and old blankets over them, and play at camps.

I was born in the December so I was 8 when the war started in 1939. The complexion of the village began to change the following year with the Bevin Boys coming in, mainly from places like London. The evacuees came later in 1940 and more came in 1941. The day the first evacuees came, a coach just turned up in the village and they moved slowly down the street knocking on doors to see if people had any space for the children who were aged anything from 7 to 14. These children were from Birmingham.

While the first influx of children was from Birmingham, we had some more later from Coventry, and also a lot from one of Dr Barnadoe's Homes in London. In fact some of these Barnadoe's children remained at the families they had stayed with after the war. They had been adopted in effect. There seemed to be a lot more organisation about the later intakes of evacuees, a coach didn't just pitch up.

We took two boys into our home from that first bus. They were both just a bit younger than me, about 8 or 9. One was named Brian, and the other, I think, was called Norman. One was from a big family and the other was an only child. His parents owned a garage in Hockley and they used to come and visit him once a month in this great big car, well, it seemed like a great big car to us. They always used to send him a letter each week with sixpence in, so he was rich as we only had a ha'penny on a Friday.

We all went to the same school, local children and evacuees. We had part time schooling then. Some of us went in the morning and some in the afternoon. They had a class at the working men's club which was quite a novelty. The teacher used the seat where the chairman of the club used to sit. The following year I went grammar school because I got my 11 plus, though how on part time schooling remains a mystery on part time schooling.

In our house there was my mother and my granddad as well as Phyllis, Gwen, Enid and me. My dad had already disappeared into the forces. My mother and Enid slept in the front room downstairs. My granddad had his own little bedroom, us girls slept in the back bedroom and the boys slept in the front bedroom. They had camp beds. We thought it was ever so good these camp beds but I bet they were uncomfortable in actual fact. I think they had been provided when they came. I'm not sure if the government made any other provision, payment and suchlike. I presume they did but I don't know.

We used to have what you'd call stodgy meals during the war, stew and dumplings. Meat was rationed so we didn't always have meat but we always had a main meal and a pudding even if it was only rice pudding. Granddad used to grow vegetables in the garden and he had part of the field out the back too. Everyone could have part of the field to grow vegetables if they wanted to. Lakins down the road used to keep pigs so when they killed one we all got a bit and the people next door used to keep chicken so we had eggs from them, so we didn't do too bad really.

The one lad, on his second day with us saw an opening in a fence to the field with some cows in and went running down to it yelling, "cows, cows." He didn't see the barbed wire across the opening and went running into it. He cut all his face so that wasn't very nice. Otherwise they fitted in quite well. The evacuees weren't with us in the village very long really. I should say it was about 18 months, then they started to trickle back home. After they went home they did keep in touch for a while, but in those days it wasn't as easy to keep in touch and I don't know what happened to them I'm sure. They could have got killed in any of the raids.

While they were with us though, we all used to play together. They came and put some Anderson Shelters up, those air raid shelters the government provided with the curved roof. All the kids used to go and play on them.

We never had any air raids. We used to hear the sirens but the planes were going over to Birmingham. We could see the barrage balloon over Birmingham and at night we could see the searchlights. We knew Birmingham was being bombed heavily and it must have affected the boys knowing that the bombs could be dropping on their homes.

My mother had to keep up mortgage payments on the house. She used to work in the munitions factory during the war. She used to make the shells at a munitions factory in Coventry. A bus used to come to the village to pick the workers up and take them in. With mom out at work it was down to my granddad to look after us kids. My granddad was a smashing bloke.

The evacuees changed the face of the village during the war. Our household, like many was to change after the war too. My father had been in the army. He had gone to France, India, Africa, all sorts of places but with my dad we were never sure if this was all true. He did come back for a short time after the war getting a job as manager of an open cast mine. One day he was showing someone something and he chopped the end of one of his fingers off. So he packed that up and became a part time taxi driver for the people who owned the Palace Theatre in Tamworth. He ended up going off with the woman from the Palace.

Edna Mitchell

FROM THE KATES HILL PRESS WEBSITE

THE KATES HILL PRESS

Is an independent publisher committed to producing short runs of fiction and social history books with a west midlands theme or by a west midlands writer.
We now also publish booklets of poetry and dialect verse by Black Country/West Midlands poets.

THE KATES HILL PRESS

Operates in the Small Press tradition in which short runs are produced on subjects the publisher believes in which conventional publishing houses cannot afford to take on.

THE KATES HILL PRESS

Believes the west midlands is an area rich in culture which local people and outsiders want to read about. Check out our links page listing poetry groups, local history groups, theatre groups, and musicians.

What is a Small Press?
Small Presses operate on the principle that a small audience is better than no audience.
The Kates Hill Press brings the tradition of providing a first platform for writers to the west midlands.

A Little Known Fact:
Walt Whitman, Virginia Woolf, T S Eliot, James Joyce, Paddy Doyle...
To name a few, were all published by Small Presses at first.

SMALL PRESS - GRAND THEMES
The Kates Hill Press produces works of substance. A Witness For Peace and Ghost Voices deal with world themes.

SOMETHING FOR EVERYONE
Most Black Country books are about nostalgia for times gone by, or about a time and place that has never existed. The Kates Hill Press has titles which look back with fondness like A Pocketful of Memories; that look back with realism like The Sportsman and The Hairy Mouse, as well as titles that are hard hitting and reflect more recent and current times like The Gulf.

VISIT www.kateshillpress.co.uk

OTHER POCKETFUL OF MEMORIES TITLES FROM THE KATES HILL PRESS

IRENE M DAVIES
A Pocketful Of Memories (Rowley) - The Rowley of the 1920s is vividly recalled. Includes 10 period photographs.
A5 comb bound book, 152 pages, £6.00 (plus 80p p&p)   ISBN 1 904552 07 2

TOSSIE PATRICK
A Pocketful Of Memories (Blackheath) - the Blackheath of the 1930s is recalled. (illustrated by Ron Slack)
A5 booklet, 32 pages, £2.50 (plus 40p p&p)   ISBN 0 9520317 3 6

RAYMOND SMOUT
A Pocketful of Memories (Coseley) - An unofficial history of Coseley, one of the Black Country's lost boroughs, prefixes some recollections of the 1960s town. With 9 photographs and 4 illustrations.
A5 booklet, 52 pages, £3.00 (plus 50p p&p)   ISBN 078 1 904552 18 5

JULIA WARING
A Pocketful Of Memories (Acocks Green) - A childhood in an abusive household in the back to backs of Acocks Green is vividly described.
A5 booklet, 52 pages, £3.00 (plus 50p p&p)   ISBN 1 904552 12 9

To order any title write to THE KATES HILL PRESS,
126 Watsons Green Road, Dudley, DY2 7LG,
cheques payable to "The Kates Hill Press"
email: kateshillpress@blueyonder.co.uk
Visit our Website: www.kateshillpress.co.uk

OTHER SOCIAL HISTORY TITLES FROM THE KATES HILL PRESS

CAROL HATHORNE
Five Minutes Love - The three volume's of national author Carol Hathorne's biography, brought together in one book. Includes Slurry and Strawberries, Bread Pudding Days, and A Woodbine On The Wall.
A5 Comb bound book, 172 pages, £6.50 (plus 80p p&p) ISBN 1 904552 13 7

BARRY MORRIS
Ghost Voices – An account of the experiences of the Vietnam War by a Royal Marine serving with the UN.
A5 paperback, 320 pages, £7.99 (plus 90p p&p)   ISBN 1 904552 01 3

GREG STOKES
A Witness For Peace - A Dudley family fight for justice following a political murder in Morocco.
A5 paperback, 176 pages, £6.99 (plus 80p p&p)   ISBN 0 9520317 1 X

JOHN SUMMERTON
My Mate StAn - John's personal odyssey as a Bluenose woven into a history of Birmingham City's St Andrew's ground. 100 years old in 2006. 5 photos.
A5 booklet, 48 pages, £3.00 (plus 40p p&p)   ISBN 1 904552 10 2

BLACK COUNTRY CLASSICS

Bringing works long out of print to the modern audience.

DUD DUDLEY
Mettallum Martis – The man who discovered how to smelt iron from coal in commercial quantities sets out the difficulties encountered in doing so.
A5 booklet, 40 pages, £3.00 (plus 40p p&p)   ISBN 1 904552 03 X

AMY LYONS
Black Country Sketches - 16 short stories written in 1905, set around Wednesbury 100 yrs before then.
A5 comb bound book, 98 pages, £5.00 (plus 70p p&p)   ISBN 1 904552 02 1